For Mum – who at 86 years is still teaching us to enjoy the adventure of our lives and remain brave, strong and true.

To our precious siblings – **Jean, Carleton, Denton, Earl & Marie** – we love each of you and your families deeply. Together we ALL carry pieces of mum's story in our hearts.

Book layout & Graphic Design by Dunja Pantic
Published by Bittersweet Symphony

Miss Mitch

& The BIG White Bird

The Story of Eutella Icilda Mitchell

Story / MAGGIE ALLEN
Illustrations / DOREEN SIBANDA
with support from Peter Kwangwara

Under the old family tree,
Miss Mitch sat
Dreaming of mangoes and sour sap.
1, 2, 3
Sitting high up in the tree
What can YOU see?

She took a **BIG** bite,
Of a bright, orange mango with juicy flesh
And imagined her face was quite a mess.
She looked up at the **hot** Jamaican sky
And squinted as the sun caught her eye.
This was her favourite place,
A space where Miss Mitch
always felt safe.

Sitting in the wash hut with her brother,
She overheard the wise words
of Frien'Mum her mother.
"Bredda Son, pay attention bwoy
Education is not a toy!
Learning your Lesson weLL
WiLL mean, you won't have to seLL
Bammy and breadfruit.
One day son, I want to see you in a suit!"

"Nyeeeerm!
Nnnnyeeeeeeerm!"

What or why
Was this rude noise coming from the sky?!

"Frien'Mum!"

Miss Mitch jumped up and ran to the wash hut

Where a pile of laundry sat.

She counted **7, 8, 9**

Some wet clothes hung on a line.

Flapping wildly, high, this way, that way,

Then falling into gentle sway

She saw the washing fall to its knees.

"Frien'Mum, look pun de bird!

He's making a sound I never heard!"

Frien'Mum looked up

But never said a word –

She could not see the BIG white bird.

The children hid behind flowery skirt
To protect themselves from being hurt.

"Pickinnini, why yuh so 'fraid
This is something that the good Lord made!"

"The school chil'en say that the exhaust
smoke in the sky means that God has come
to judge us!"
Miss Mitch cried.

"**STOP** with all this fuss,"
Frien'Mum reassured.
"Nutting nuh go so. It's an aeroplane,
see it a go."
She swished her hand towards the sky
And let out a deep, hefty sigh.
"Pickinnies, understan'
Planes **mus'** fly across de lan'.
Picking up people at different stations
To take them to their various destinations.
Cum now, go wash ya face
Set de table, a time fe grace."

Some days went by
And Miss Mitch had her eyes
peeled to the sky.
From her favourite spot she lay
And counted mangoes, **3**
Growing nicely from the tree.
In the kitchen Frien'Mum was
preparing her favourite dish
Dumplings, ackee and salt fish.

"Miss Mitch, what you a do?"
She turned to meet a voice she knew.
Sitting close at her feet
Bredda Son Asked, "Ya'avin fun?"
"De mangoes, soon ripe" she said
"And then I will take a juicy bite
– of that one."
And pointed towards the sun.

"Nyeeeerm,
Nnnnyeeeeeerm!"
The sound got Louder,
Louder and Louder.

Smoky clouds filled the air
Like powder.
"Ooooh," said Miss Mitch,
eyes open wide.
She searched around
for somewhere to hide.
"Now, now, Little Titch,"
Bredda Son said,
"It's not judgement day.
Remember what Frien'Mum say.
It's an aeroplane
That's what it name."

Frien'Mum was **taller** than most
She always was a perfect host.
She was friendly,
that's how she got her name
Her laughter alone brought her much fame.
A mother no-one could mistreat
With broad shoulders and size **8** feet.
Old John, her husband
was short and revealed
His daily passion for working the field.
Both parents gave their children their best
They were proud each time they passed their tests.

3 of her brothers had plans for England
That green and pleasant place
Where harsh weather tore at the face.
There the ground was covered in snow
A white foam that would come and go.
For Miss Mitch, Frien'Mum was her **world**
Ever since she was a little girl.

Would she one day travel on a plane-
That white looking bird with a funny name?
Bredda Son said,
it takes people here and there
That people actually travel
through the air!
Over houses, over land,
Over sea and over sand.

He said "One day, you and me
Will move away from this mango tree."
"What on earth, do you mean?
Miss Mitch had asked.
"As for me, I would never dream
Of leaving Frien'Mum.
Who would put my hair in a bun?"

Bredda Son chuckled and said
"Don't worry your little head,
Frien'Mum will be just fine
She will manage over time."

Miss Mitch was now 24
And who could really ask for more?
With her face pressed against the window
She remembered her mango tree
And wondered "Is it missing me?"
She stroked the crisp collar
Of her dress, just 4 Jamaican dollar –
Quite a bargain that's for sure.

She counted the flowers,
2, 3, 4
Frien'Mum had sown
Six dresses with buttons and bows.
As she thought of her mother,
her heart grew heavy and sad
She missed her so much,
as well as her dad.

But there she sat
With her small red hat
On a big white boat
Passport in hand, pulling on her coat.
She had arrived in a foreign land
The one and only England.

Her brothers were already there
They had earned money to pay their fare.
She was scared. Who would have dared
Or imagined this day
When tea would be served to her on a plastic tray?!
Engine **roaring**,
Rain **a pouring**.
The ground beneath her feet
Boasted no heat,
Her heart skipped a beat.

"What were these people like?
Would the days look like night?"

She told herself to relax
And smoothed her hair with creamy Dax.
As she thought of the man of her dreams
Whom she would shortly marry, it seems
He said, "You will be my wife.
I promise you a better life."

"England, is it the place for me?
No more sitting under the mango tree.
No more strife
No more hard life?"

"They say the 'streets are paved with gold'
that people here live 'til they're old."
So much thought!
Will she remember all she was taught?
What did Frien'Mum say
"Miss Mitch, work hard, promises keep
And **many** blessing you will reap!"

The gushing ocean gave her comfort
"Gurgle, **gurgle**, **gurgle**,"
it went as the waves hit the boat
Miss Mitch shuddered and buttoned her coat.

The boat had landed
Passport handed
Air was crisp
Families kiss
Hugs, shouts of laughter
Plenty smiles and
Lots of happy ever afters.

"Ce-Ce
It's me!
Miss Mitch.
Little Titch."
His Trousers baggy and **big**
Big enough to do a jig.
Dresses all Jamaican colours
Jamaican sounds
Swelled in the port all around.
It was like a colour invasion
As Jamaica flooded the UK nation.

Sea faded all around
"Hello, my new English ground."
People of colour
Stared hard at the dull landscape.
Many heads shake.
This must be a **HUGE** mistake!

"My dear mango tree - farewell!
We have many stories to tell.
But not now.
We must first find out how
To curtesy and to bow
When we stand before the queen.
Is her favourite colour, blue or green?"

Marse Ce took her hand,
"Welcome to this pleasant land.
This is your new life
And soon you will be my cherished wife.
Today we will tour the sights
I'll show you the city highlights."

Miss Mitch left the dock
In her colourful Jamaican frock
Already the familiar smells
Faded like church bells.
The smell of curry chicken
Fried in the outdoor Jamaican kitchen.
Smell of laboured hand
"Farewell, Jamaican land!"
Smell of field sweat,
"Farewell, my Jamaican sunset!"

"Frien'Mum, where are you?
Wah me fe do?
I want to go home, set the sail
Bring me my rag and pail.
I miss my washing line

Counting clothes 7, 8, 9
I've exchanged my mango tree
For a land of English tea,
Of bread and butter
Streets with gutter
Cobbled stones
And cold bones.
Fish and chips
Suitcase and grips
English people
Churches, steeple."

Eyes that stare
Eyes that glare
Eyes that **flare**
Eyes that **tear!**

Miss Mitch was home sick
And held tightly to her grip.
"New life?
New wife?
London streets are cold
And where,
O where is the gold?"

Marse Ce took her by the hand as they waited
To see the Queen from the gate.
The new Queen is here and its 1953
Pictures of British Queen
She had all her life seen,
But to have the new queen
Before her was more than a dream.
"We might see her, how funny
It would be if she came to the balcony."
Suddenly, flags waving high,
"Long live the Queen!" people cry.
"She's here, she's here!"
The crowds give out a loud cheer.

From Buckingham Palace to
Houses of Parliament;
Big Ben to
Westminster Abbey
Miss Mitch was ever so happy.
As long as she held onto Marse Ce
She tried to forget about the Caribbean sun
And how she used to wear her hair in a bun.

Frien'Mum's voice kept flowing through her head
"Miss Mitch, mek sure yuh stay well fed
Keep yuh house clean
And never be mean
Always give what you can to those in need –
That's the life you must lead."

"Farewell, Frien'Mum, I love you so
I love you more than you will know
I will write to you and send you word
And visit you soon in a Big White Bird."

MAGGIE ALLEN (Gigi) is a seasoned London based writer and wordsmith who has been penning and performing stories since her youth. Born in the 1960s to Jamaican parents who left their homeland in search of a better life in England, she is one of seven children who spent her childhood living in the East Midlands. Today Maggie is happily married with four grown up children and nine amazing grandchildren who are as colourful as the rainbow. She has vast experience in social work empowering vulnerable communities and also prides herself in being a committed Christian with an enduring passion for evangelism and local and international missions.

DOREEN SIBANDA is a passionate and acclaimed mixed media painter and curator who has lived her way around art since she was a little girl. The eldest of seven children born in the UK to Jamaican parents, she trained as an art teacher during which time she honed her artistic skills. Her surreal mixed media approach to art making has brought her work to audiences in Russia, Czech Republic, Sweden and Zimbabwe. Doreen currently serves as the Executive Director of the National Gallery of Zimbabwe since 2004, an institution she has worked for, for some twenty years. A wife, a mother and doting grandmother, she spends her time writing about art and attending to her home

19577347R00032

Printed in Poland
by Amazon Fulfillment
Poland Sp. z o.o., Wrocław